**THE BLUEPRINT FOR A CULTURE OF ENGAGEMENT,
OWNERSHIP AND BOTTOM-LINE PERFORMANCE**

Culture
in

TONY MOORE
THE CULTURE ARCHITECT

Published by Richter Publishing LLC
www.richterpublishing.com

Book Cover Design: Jessie Alarcon

Editors: Savannah Grooms, Monica San Nicolas, Georgiana Tudor, Rachel Meldrum, Margarita Martinez & Natalie Meyer

Proofreader: Nastassia Clarke

ISBN-10: 1945812192

ISBN-13: 978-1945812194

DISCLAIMER

This book is designed to provide information on business culture only. This information is provided and sold with the knowledge that the publisher and author do not offer any legal or medical advice. In the case of a need for any such expertise, consult with the appropriate professional. This book does not contain all information available on the subject. This book has not been created to be specific to any individual person or organization's situation or needs. Reasonable efforts have been made to make this book as accurate as possible. However, there may be typographical and or content errors. Therefore, this book should serve only as a general guide. This book contains information that might be dated or erroneous and is intended only to educate and entertain. The author and publisher shall have no liability or responsibility to any person or entity regarding any loss or damage incurred, or alleged to have incurred, directly or indirectly, by the information contained in this book or as a result of anyone acting or failing to act upon the information in this book. You hereby agree never to sue and to hold the author and publisher harmless from any and all claims arising out of the information contained in this book. You hereby agree to be bound by this disclaimer, covenant not to sue and release. You may return this book within the guaranteed time period for a full refund. In the interest of full disclosure, this book contains affiliate links that might pay the author or publisher a commission upon any purchase from the company. While the author and publisher take no responsibility for any virus or technical issues that could be caused by such links, the business practices of these companies, and or the performance of any product or service, the author or publisher has used the product or service and makes a recommendation in good faith based on that experience. All characters appearing in this work are fictitious. Any resemblance to real persons, living or dead, is purely coincidental. The opinions and stories in this book are the views of the author and not that of the publisher.

DEDICATION

This book is dedicated to my bride, Aundra Moore. Thank you for your unending support and serving as a model of patience, grace, and encouragement. By doing so, you have made me a better husband, father, and leader. I thank God for you.

TABLE OF CONTENTS

ACKNOWLEDGEMENTS

David Dennis, President and CEO of Eckerd Connects. Over the course of the last thirty years, you have been a source of inspiration, encouragement, and support. Proverbs 27:17 reads, "As iron sharpens iron, so one person sharpens another." Thank you for sharpening me. I am a better person and professional because of you.

Bridgette Simmonds, my executive coach. The timing of our paths crossing was by God's design. I was at a crossroads and you challenged my thinking and encouraged my heart. Your intervention enabled me to break through barriers, making starting my business and writing this book a reality.

Melissa Robinson, past president of HR Tampa. You have no idea the role our monthly lunch meetings had in making "Tony Moore Speaks" and writing this book a reality. Thank you for your encouragement and believing I could do it long before I did.

The greatest team I have ever had the privilege of leading.
Tracy Willis, Ryan Byrd, Keith Gauthier, Crystal Barwick, Brandie Holjes, Candy Ravenstein, Margie James, Rob Painter, Marie McBride, Pat Girdner, and Mary Beth Davis. Thank you for

teaching me how to lead.

Owners & baristas at The Grindhouse, Clearwater, FL. Thank you for allowing me to camp out at your café and keeping me caffeinated as I wrote this book.

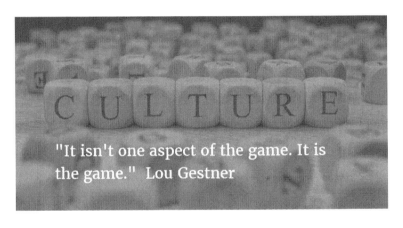

"It isn't one aspect of the game. It is the game." Lou Gestner

Figure 1. Picture credit deposit photos, meme created by Tony Moore.

INTRODUCTION

In the 1987-88 season, the Detroit Pistons faced the Los Angeles Lakers in the NBA Finals. The Lakers were there to defend their title, while the Pistons were attempting to win the first championship in franchise history. No one would argue that both the Lakers and Pistons weren't high-performing teams. Simply making it to the finals was confirmation of that fact. Yes, these were the two best teams in the NBA that year, and only a best of seven series would determine who was the champion. Like many finals series, this one went the distance, with the Lakers emerging victorious, successfully defending their title. The Pistons returned to Detroit as the second-best team in the NBA.

As Detroit's point guard, Isiah Thomas, tells the story, it was a very painful offseason. The thought of coming that close to being champions and falling short weighed heavily on him. Isiah, who had won an NCAA Championship at Indiana University, was unaccustomed to being on the losing end of a series.

In the summer of 1988, following the loss to the Lakers, Isiah learned that fellow teammates Bill Laimbeer and Joe Dumars were also experiencing a deep sense of loss. The three made a pact that summer; they would put in the work necessary to get back to the NBA Finals, and anyone on the team who did not want it as badly as the three of them had to go! The evaluation of each player's level of commitment would be based on what they did, not what they said.

At the conclusion of the 1988-89 season, the Pistons returned to the NBA Finals, where they would once again face the Lakers. For the Lakers, it was an opportunity to make history by becoming only one of three teams to win three championships in a row. For the Pistons, it was an opportunity to avenge their loss from the previous year and secure the franchise's first championship. Unlike the previous year, the tables would turn in favor of the Pistons. They would emerge victorious by sweeping the Lakers four games to zero, effectively accomplishing the very thing they had committed to the summer before. The Pistons would go on to win another championship the following year.

A championship sports team, like any other high-performing team, does not get there by accident. Those teams that rise to the top of their game, outpacing and outperforming their peers, tend to have three things in common, all of which the Pistons possessed: vision, behavior, and commitment.

1. They committed to a common vision—winning an NBA championship.

2. They committed to a set of behaviors necessary to accomplish their vision.

3. They refused to have anyone on the team whose behavior did not demonstrate his commitment to the vision.

Essentially, they created a culture with clearly defined rules of engagement and made protecting that culture the highest priority.

Consistently delivering results begins with a common vision that everyone on a team understands, agrees to, and takes ownership for accomplishing. This vision or goal serves as a sort of North Star, used by a team for navigation. It is a point of reference that lets them know when they are on track, off track, or in danger of drifting.

Southwest Airlines, which has grown to be one of America's premier airlines, was founded in 1971 with the intent of providing service to three cities in Texas—Dallas, Houston, and San Antonio. From the beginning, their vision was clear: deliver exemplary customer service while keeping prices low. Being the leading low-cost carrier was an element of the vision they took very seriously, leading to several strategic decisions focused on maintaining that status.

When I was in graduate school, my professor shared a story of an alleged conversation between Southwest Airlines' founder, Herb Kelleher, and one of his senior leaders. It demonstrates how seriously they took the goal of being the premier low-cost carrier.

> *Sr. Leader:* "Now that we're providing longer flights, we should consider serving meals instead of peanuts. I think it would improve the customer experience."

> *Kelleher:* "That's a great suggestion. Let me ask you a question. Is it possible to serve meals while remaining a low-cost carrier?"

> *Sr. Leader:* "Serving meals would definitely affect fares."

> *Kelleher:* "Well, then, you have your answer."

I am not sure if this is a true story or part of the mythology of Herb Kelleher and Southwest Airlines. It does, however, demonstrate the power of a clearly articulated vision that everyone understands, agrees to, and takes ownership for accomplishing.

Every year, organizations invest millions of dollars in strategic planning and software to track execution. Senior leaders spend countless hours in training sessions to increase competency and learn the next great approach to leadership. Ping pong tables, video games, and massage chairs are installed to make work feel... well, less like work. This is all part of a quest to fulfill an organization's mission, with the goal of gaining a competitive advantage.

In and of themselves, these are all worthwhile endeavors. Unfortunately, they often fall short of expectations for one fundamental reason: culture. You see, no amount of planning, training, or even beanbag chairs can overcome a badly constructed culture. Engaging in these activities without any focus on the culture necessary to support them is like planting seeds without first preparing the soil. If you're lucky, a few flowers will spring up; however, if you want a garden you can be proud of, you better start by working on the soil. In other words, fail to get the culture right, and nothing else will matter.

Maurice's Story

Many years ago, I was working with an operations director, who we will refer to as Maurice. Maurice's voluntary turnover was twice that of all other operations directors in the company. When I spoke with him about his turnover, he talked about the difficulty of finding employees who could keep pace and meet his high expectations, younger employees who did not want to pay their dues but wanted everything given to them, and the fact that sometimes people just needed to go.

I mentioned to him that a good body of research seems to indicate people do not leave organizations, they leave people. He indicated his agreement, suggesting that his high standards were, perhaps, the reason employees often left him. I told him that most certainly could be the case. However, in the event that there were additional reasons, I suggested we review the exit survey data on employees who had left voluntarily over the past 18 months, followed by a survey of his current employees regarding the culture of the team. To my surprise, he agreed.

In the exit survey, most employees indicated that they had left for more money, more opportunities for growth, or personal reasons. In the comments, however, there were three common themes:

1. There were cliques on the team, with long-term employees making it hard for new employees to integrate.

2. There was a definite "this is the way we have always done it" approach to the work, making it hard for new people to make a contribution.

3. What they believed to be true about the organization (the reason they had joined) and what they experienced on the team

were not the same.

The most telling response was the number of people who, when asked, "Would you return to work at this company in the future?" answered, "Yes, as long as I am on a different team."

Although Maurice had seen the data before, he had always been able to explain it away based on who he believed was making the comments. He, like many leaders, was very confident on the surface and good at convincing people he was right. In spite of his high turnover, he always hit his targets by the end of the year, so everyone believed him and backed off. With a little pushing, however, he was willing to admit there were problems, and he really wasn't sure how to change the culture of his team.

He committed to allowing me to dig deeper, in an effort to help him design and build a culture of ownership that would increase engagement, decrease turnover, and exceed business targets. Later in the book, I will share more about the work we did.

Why I Wrote This Book

Over the course of the last 30 years, I have had the privilege of designing and building multiple team cultures, as well as leading the cultural integration of multiple mergers. I have led teams that have been wildly successful, and I have led teams that have failed miserably. I have had teams of highly talented individuals who never produced the expected results, and I have had teams with less talent who rarely, if ever, missed the mark.

I have reflected on the factors that differentiated my truly great teams from those that were less than stellar, and I have come to realize that outside of the impact of my shortcomings as a leader, the tipping point was always the culture of the team. When our values were all aligned and our behavior toward one another supported those values, our performance soared. On the other hand, when there was a mismatch between what we said we believed and how we treated each other, our performance suffered. Additionally, there appeared to be a correlation between mismatched behavior and values and the amount of tension, stress, and staff turnover.

Something else I realized was that the more intentional and deliberate we were in defining our values and their associated behaviors, the more likely we were to see consistency between the two. As consistency increased, so did trust and performance. My most successful teams outlined a set of values by which they would live, backed them up with very specific behaviors we called Rules of Engagement, and then took ownership for protecting the culture. By taking their beliefs about what makes a great team from concept to action, I have watched previously struggling teams outperform their counterparts throughout the organization.

As mentioned previously, I have led the cultural integration of multiple mergers. In all cases, our success or failure in producing the results we anticipated at the beginning of the deal rested in our ability to integrate cultures. In the words of Lou Gerstner, former turnaround CEO at IBM, "Culture isn't just one aspect of the game; it *is* the game."

The goal of this book is not only to make the case for approaching team culture as a business imperative, but to also share some of the basic tools I use in my work as a Culture Architect. I am going to provide you with a blueprint for a culture of engagement, ownership, and bottom-line performance by introducing you to the "Tony Moore Speaks 4D System."

Throughout the book, I will be challenging you to demonstrate your belief that culture is important by taking steps with your team to intentionally and deliberately create a culture of excellence. I will be inviting you to combat the plague of employee disengagement by engaging your employees in a process where they will Dream, Design, Develop, and Defend the culture they desire.

Rather than leaving the outcome up to you alone, *Culture in*

4D empowers you and your team to take ownership for the employee experience. What does, however, rest squarely on your shoulders is the responsibility of making culture a priority. In my experience, great teams do not require a leader to hold them accountable because the members of the team have taken ownership for business outcomes. Designing and building a culture in which behaviors are aligned with beliefs is the most critical step in the pursuit of a culture of ownership.

Figure 2. Picture credit deposit photos. Quote & picture meme created by Tony Moore.

CHAPTER 1

CULTURE MATTERS

Peter Drucker is famously quoted as saying, "Culture eats strategy for breakfast." I would also add lunch and dinner to the menu. In fact, there is no facet of an organization that is more important than its culture.

I always experience a great deal of stress on the morning of my keynotes. So when I was scheduled to speak at a conference in Sarasota, Florida, less than 60 miles from my home in Clearwater, I decided I would go down the night before to both reduce the chances of something going wrong and to allow me a traffic-free, dare I say, stress-free, morning before the presentation.

As a Hilton Honors member, I debated whether to stay at a hotel in the Hilton chain or in the Holiday Inn, which was connected to the conference site. With the goal of wanting to reduce stress, I reluctantly chose the Holiday Inn.

The next morning after I completed my workout, I went to the hotel restaurant for breakfast. I stepped up to the counter and was asked by a nice enough gentleman if I would be having the buffet or ordering from the menu. I selected from the menu and he instructed me to take a seat anywhere that looked comfortable.

After about five minutes of reviewing the menu, I looked up to see if I could get the attention of the waitstaff. I saw a few people swarming around, so I continued to wait patiently. After five more minutes and having several waiters pass me without any acknowledgement, I managed to get one's attention.

"Excuse me, sir," I said, "I am ordering from the menu. Do I order at my table, or do I go back up to the counter?"

He said, "You order at the table," and walked off. He did not take my order, nor did he tell me he would send someone to assist me. He simply answered my question and walked away.

After a few more minutes, I saw this same gentleman emerge from the back and speak to one of the other waiters. I was not within earshot; however, I am certain I read his lips as he said, "You have a customer at one of your tables." This waiter then walked right past me, made a comment to the couple behind me, and disappeared. So much for a stress-free morning!

I sat there even longer in utter disbelief and then thought, "There has to be someplace better than this to eat." I Googled breakfast restaurants near me and noticed there was a Hilton Garden Inn three miles to the south. I jumped in the car and drove directly there.

As I entered the hotel, the lady behind the reservation counter looked up, smiled, and said, "Good morning, sir."

I headed over to the restaurant, and a waitress who was cleaning a table looked up and said, "Good morning, sir. Have a seat, and I will be right with you." Moments later, I had a hot cup of coffee and was engaged in a discussion with the waitress about how cool she thought my shoes were. I exhaled deeply; I was home!

Interestingly enough, the Hilton Garden Inn wasn't the only place that came up during my search. There were several restaurants from which to select. I chose the Hilton Garden Inn, perhaps an odd choice for breakfast considering it's a hotel, not a restaurant, because I knew what to expect. I knew from my many travels that they would make me feel right at home!

The great companies build great cultures. Think of Southwest Airlines, Starbucks, or the Ritz Carlton. These are all establishments whose employees' actions toward their customers are reflective of the culture of the organization. Without creating a culture where respect is valued, training an employee to treat your customers with respect is like expecting a bird to fly after its wings have been clipped. Culture is the soil in which everything in the organization lives or dies!

Once, I was contacted by a CEO who was concerned that her middle managers were not strategic enough in their thinking. She indicated their decisions were far too myopic, failing to take into consideration the bigger picture. Her hope was that I could provide some training to assist them. I asked her if she had any sense as to the root cause, and she stated it could be competency or lack of experience, which was why she thought training was the appropriate intervention.

I suggested I start by interviewing each manager individually, as well as the entire group, in order to gather data that would help us design the training. As one can imagine, the interviews were very informative. Three themes emerged which appeared to point to an issue that was far different from the one originally presented by the CEO. The managers were forthcoming with information and their explanation of the cause.

Managers: "We don't understand the way our day-to-day work connects to the organization's broader vision. It's like putting together a jigsaw puzzle without knowing what the final picture looks like."

Cause: "Vision and direction-related decisions only occur at the executive level of the organization, and then we are simply told what to do."

Managers: "Decisions are made with no input from us, and we are expected to execute them. Our contributions are undervalued. It's as if they don't trust us. We are always the last ones to be fully informed."

Cause: "Information is hoarded, and then slowly trickles down to us."

Managers: "We always feel like we are off schedule and operating with unrealistic timelines. There is no time to plan."

Cause: "Like everything else, by the time we have enough information to make a decision, we're expected to have already completed the first two or three steps on the execution path."

Training this group to improve its strategic thinking skills would have been a waste of time and money; seeds would have failed to take root because their issue was in the soil. The issue was one of culture.

Culture "... shapes the way people make decisions, get their work done, what they prioritize, and how they interact with colleagues, clients, and customers" (Newton, 2016). In my experience, we are far too quick to identify an underperforming employee, incompetent manager, or poor system as the issue, when in fact the true culprit is embedded in the culture in which these individuals have been asked to operate.

Culture, Performance, and Research

After studying over 2,000 private and public companies in 60 countries, The Barrett Values Centre concluded that there's a strong link between financial performance and alignment between an organization's values and the personal values of its employees (Barrett, 2011). Take Chick-fil-A as an example. They have experienced the kind of success that most restaurants only dream of. Since launching in 1946, they have had a 10% sales increase almost every year. Their franchisees' retention rate has been 96% for nearly 50 years, with a corporate staff retention rate at 95-97% during the same period (Kruse, 2015).

In *Corporate Culture and Performance,* John Kotter and James Heskett found that companies whose employees shared their values had a profit ratio 750 times higher than those who did not. As further evidence of this, a multi-decade study conducted by Jim Collins and Jerry Porras, documented in their book *Built to*

Last, concluded that companies with a values-driven culture outperform competitors by a factor of six. These same companies outperform the general stock market by a factor of fifteen.

A study conducted by Nathaniel J. Williams and Charles Glisson (2014) found that organizational culture has a direct impact on employee and organizational performance, as well as clients served. Additionally, in their review of current literature, Smith, Peters, and Caldwell (2016) posited that a culture of engagement is necessary to foster innovation, profitability, and improve overall organizational quality.

Organizations with clearly stated values, whose behavior is aligned with those values, outperform those who do not. Financial outcomes, quality service delivery, operational excellence, and superior product creation can all be linked back to culture. When we pursue a common goal with a group of people with whom we share values, we are willing to work harder, longer, and take on herculean tasks, all while looking out for one another. At the end of the day, culture matters!

Figure 3. Picture credit deposit photos. Picture meme created by Tony Moore.

CHAPTER 2

OWNERSHIP OR ACCOUNTABILITY

Early in my career, I operated with the belief that one of the fundamental roles of a leader was holding people accountable. "You have to hold them accountable" is what I was frequently told, so holding my team accountable became my primary goal. Perhaps you currently believe holding people accountable is one of your core responsibilities. If you are like me, you did not pull this belief out of midair, you learned it from the leaders who shaped you.

Over the years, I have come to appreciate the value of ownership over accountability, a viewpoint I adopted after failing as a leader. I feel so strongly about the subject that I frequently speak and write about the commonly accepted myth that people must be held accountable. I occasionally encounter people who disagree with me. However, even if you believe you can actually hold people accountable, should you have to? Do you really want to?

I, like you, have heard it all before: "holding people accountable comes with the territory" or "if you do not hold people accountable, they won't respect you." To be honest , I have a hard enough time holding myself accountable, so it should come as no surprise when I tell you that eventually I failed miserably at holding people accountable.

At one point in my career, I was recruited to lead the turnaround of a struggling business development department. The previous leader had apparently struggled with holding people accountable, and the CEO had been told I was the person for the job. Within a six to nine month period, our team showed real progress. So much progress, in fact, that after 12 months I was asked to take over another department. Once again, the issue was one of accountability.

Now I had two teams under my leadership. Fortunately, I was continually present since all of the employees had offices in the same hallway, therefore my "holding everyone accountable" worked. To this day, I am amazed we were successful, but we were. Both teams hit their targets for the year, and my CEO once again praised my ability to hold people accountable.

To ensure no good deed went unpunished, my CEO asked me to take over a third department that was in need of, wait for it ... accountability. It was at this point that the wheels started to come off the bus.

About three months into leadership of this final team, I started to feel like Andrew Van Buren, the famous plate spinner.

Figure 4. Plate spinner. http://www.vanburen.org.uk

I spent so much of my time running from department to department holding people accountable that I wasn't able to lead. There was no time for planning, no time for system improvements, and no time to be strategic. To top it all off, our performance slipped significantly.

Now before you assume the issue was too many employees to supervise, let me share that I have not only supervised more employees, I have successfully supervised teams in multiple states. My failure was rooted in flawed thinking. Instead of being responsible for holding people accountable, I needed to be responsible for hiring employees who would hold themselves accountable. I needed a culture of ownership, not the rod of accountability. Allow me to illustrate the difference.

My family and I are the proud owners of two great dogs, a Boxer named Toby and a Lab/Rottweiler mix named Maggie. Whenever my wife and I leave the house for an extended period of time, we text my 17-year-old son, reminding him to feed the dogs. My son cares about the well-being of our dogs; however, we still have to take steps to ensure he is accountable for taking care of them. On the other hand, when my wife leaves the house, she doesn't text me to feed Toby and Maggie. It's not necessary, because I have taken ownership for the well-being of our pets.

Consequently, I have long since given up trying to hold people accountable. When the members of my team have accountability that emerges from within, our success skyrockets. The truly great teams are defined by the degree to which everyone on the team takes ownership for the culture and business outcomes. I still use the word accountability. However, when I do, I am referring to reporting systems for tracking progress, making course corrections, and ensuring the right work is getting done at the right time. I no longer have to look over anyone's shoulder or need to follow up multiple times. A culture of ownership is far more powerful and effective than a leader spending her time trying to hold people accountable.

QUESTIONS FOR REFLECTION

Do you believe ownership differs from accountability? Why or why not?

Is your team best described as one where people have taken ownership for performance outcomes or a team where someone holds them accountable for performance outcomes?

What one action could you take to increase the sense of ownership on your team?

What one action could you take to demonstrate your ownership for the team's culture?

CULTURE IN 4D

Figure 5. Picture credit deposit photos. Meme created by Tony Moore.

Chapter 3

DIAGNOSING THE DISCONNECT

"People are our greatest asset" is an often quoted mantra by organizational leaders. You would be hard pressed to find anyone who could claim success without referencing the people who delivered the results. Nevertheless, in 2016, the Gallup Organization reminded us that 50.8% of U.S. employees are not engaged, with 17.2% actively disengaged (defined as involved in activities to sabotage the efforts of their organizations). (Adkins, 2016).

CEOs speak with such high regard for employees, yet a survey of employees in 2015 concluded 21% of respondents planned to find a new employer in 2016 (Soergel, 2015). What is the cause of the disconnect?

I believe the cause of the disconnect can be found in a quote from a 2016 article from the *Harvard Business Review*: "Business leaders believe a strong organization culture is critical to success, yet ... most executives manage it according to their intuition." Culture, which has a direct impact on employees and performance, is being left up to the "gut feeling" of executives.

For the record, I do not believe executives are solely responsible for an organization's culture. As a matter of fact, in the best organizations, all employees take ownership for creating and sustaining a healthy culture. Nevertheless, as a former executive, I believe we have a responsibility to set the right tone for the organization's culture. In the words of Uncle Ben to Spiderman, "With great power comes great responsibility."

I believe the tendency to "... manage it according to their intuition" speaks to a lack of knowledge about designing and developing a healthy corporate culture versus a disregard for its importance. The reality is "Very few companies intentionally work on their culture—in fact, many companies just let culture happen" (Osterwalder, Pigneur, and Guppta, 2016).

No CFO would ever say, "Let's forgo budget and financial records this year. We have great employees. I'm certain they won't overspend." What chief quality officer would ever advise the CEO, "Our people know what they are doing. Let's not waste our time with metrics or a continuous quality improvement process. We can trust them"? No chief human resources officer would ever say, "Who needs policies? Given a choice between right and wrong, people will always choose right." In all of the above cases, intentionality is critical, as a failure in one of these areas can sink an organization. By having systems in place, we demonstrate their importance and level of priority.

Because culture is the soil in which everything in your organization lives or dies, it is a mistake to leave it in the hands of the well-intended. Culture must be given the same priority as finance, quality, marketing, and talent management. Furthermore, I would argue that a focus on culture is a surefire method for getting the best out of employees in the finance, quality, marketing, and talent management divisions.

Let us be clear before we go any further. Leading a culture change is not for the faint of heart. It is a process, as opposed to a check-the-box event. Progress is slow, and resistance is strong, as old habits are hard to break once they have been ingrained. Nevertheless, to the brave go the spoils! If you want a culture of engagement, ownership, and bottom-line performance, then you must do the hard work of enduring what Daniel Chambliss (1989) calls "the mundanity of excellence."

In his study of what sets a champion Olympic swimmer apart from the crowd, Daniel Chambliss (1989) concluded it is a willingness to do the mundane over and over again to attain a level of excellence. Superior performance is the result of a "complex set of discrete actions ... manageable steps which lead to qualitative differences."

Olympic champions know they are responsible for their own outcomes and as such, they are willing to endure the mundane. The creation of a great team starts by making culture a top priority, a business imperative addressed through a set of deliberate and intentional steps.

The Tony Moore Speaks 4D System is designed to help leaders and teams improve bottom-line performance by creating a culture of engagement and ownership. Based on research and real-life experience, this system pulls back the curtain to reveal the secret of building a strong and healthy team culture. The 4D System involves four phases:

1. Dream It
2. Design It
3. Develop It
4. Defend It

In addition, every member of a team will be engaged in the process, thereby creating universal buy-in.

Let's begin!

QUESTIONS FOR REFLECTION

What three words or phrases best describe your current team culture?

For each word or phrase you identified above, identify a specific behavior.

If you were going to design a team culture in which you would thrive (be your best personally and professionally), what three words or phrases would you use to describe your design?

How do your answers differ between question one and question three?

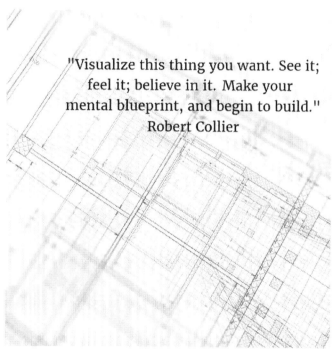

"Visualize this thing you want. See it; feel it; believe in it. Make your mental blueprint, and begin to build."
Robert Collier

Figure 6. Photo credit deposit photos. Meme created by Tony Moore

CHAPTER 4

DREAM IT

My son Parker is an artist. At 15, while attending St. Petersburg College, he was in an art competition which led to his piece being featured in the Leepa-Rattner Museum of Art. It was a proud moment for our entire family.

At one point, I asked him about the process of creating the piece and he said, "It took extreme visualization before I ever put pencil to paper." His statement made complete sense to me. Visualization is such a powerful component for any successful venture. A basketball player sees the ball entering the hoop before she shoots a free throw. A high jumper sees himself clearing the bar before he takes a step. Musicians hear a piece of music in their heads before they start to compose, and play directors block scenes mentally long before giving actors instructions. I doubt Michelangelo started painting the Sistine Chapel without visualizing what he wanted to create. And what about the Eiffel Tower, Seattle's Space Needle, or even the

Golden Gate Bridge? My guess is someone dreamed each of them long before an architect put pencil to paper.

Every great work of art, beautiful building, or well-organized kitchen started as a visualization, a dream in someone's mind. The first phase in the process of creating a culture of ownership, engagement, and bottom-line performance is to Dream It: to imagine the possibilities.

Figure 7. "One in the Same" by Parker Moore, Instagram.com/NXS_Art

The Birth of the 4D System

Although I had utilized parts of this system throughout my career, the formal system came together for me when I was appointed chief human resources officer for a large nonprofit organization in Clearwater, Florida. It was here that I began to visualize the possibilities of a team focused on engagement and ownership. My HR team was loaded with talent, but plagued by a culture of divisions, lack of clear direction, and no unifying purpose. As is often the case in situations like this, the team had disintegrated into factions, with everyone looking out for their own best interests or the interests of those in their particular group.

In an organization that desperately needed a strong talent management and development function, we were not positioned to contribute to the organization's success. Again, this was not because of a lack of talent. As a matter of fact, some of the most talented people I've worked with were on that team. The fundamental issue was one of team culture.

MATTERS OF CULTURE
Culture issues often mask themselves as employee issues. Unfortunately, we are far too quick to assume the problem is an employee, when in fact, he or she is a symptom of the problem, not the problem itself.

Now, in light of our performance, I could have started cleaning house. There were plenty of issues on which we could have focused. In addition to our internal issues, we weren't respected within the organization; people complained that we were slow to respond to requests, and when we did, we often made them duplicate their efforts because we would misplace paperwork. The department was full of drama, and it was clear there were ringleaders who kept everyone stirred up. Nevertheless, I believed if we could change the culture, we could change the outcomes.

Maurice's Story Revisited

If you recall Maurice from the introduction, he had a significantly higher turnover rate than his peers throughout the company. Someone would leave, and then Maurice would replace them. That person would last six months, leave, and then Maurice would replace them. It was a pattern that had gone on for a long time. But because he hit his numbers every year, no one questioned his explanation for the turnover.

The root cause of Maurice's issue was one of culture. He continued to hire people while expecting a different result. This fairly common response to turnover is like being told your tires are wearing out because the car is no longer aligned properly, and your response is to buy more expensive tires. The quality of tires is not the issue, alignment is.

Maurice's situation is not that uncommon in organizations. As they should be, organizations are performance- and outcomes-focused. Unfortunately, many organizations are missing the mark, valuing outcomes over how the people charged with delivering the outcomes are treated. If, of course, you are in an organization that states, "We value performance and outcomes above all things," and "we do not care how we treat you," then you know what you are getting into when you sign on the dotted line. Unfortunately, in many cases, the stated values are not aligned with the way people are treated. As an example, many organizations tout values such as respect, people first, and work-life balance while recognizing and rewarding those who have high performance but also work the longest hours and take the fewest vacation days. Notably, this often results in an inordinately emotional cost for those who are taxed to work with the virtuous employee. How many times have you heard, "James is a pain in the butt, but he gets the work done," or "that is just how Rosita is. Don't take it personally; she treats everyone that way"? The missed opportunity occurs when employees are allowed to violate the organization's values because their performance is stellar. Trading values for profit may bring short-term rewards, but the long-term issues created will one day hit like a tsunami.

Even in the story of Maurice, he initially came to my attention not because of his high turnover, but because his turnover was affecting his budget. Today I remain convinced that absent the budget impact, the status quo would have never been challenged.

So Where Do We Begin?

Knowing one has a culture issue and knowing how to fix it are two different things. The fundamental goal of the Dream It phase is to get the team thinking about what can be. To borrow from Edward de Bono's *Six Thinking Hats*, this is a Green Hat process as it focuses on possibilities, alternatives, and new ideas. Everyone must resist the natural inclination to filter out suggestions and ideas during the Dream It phase. This is especially tempting to do when members of the team have worked together for an extended period of time. The more familiar team members are with one another, the greater the tendency to think or say things such as, "Well, there is no reason to make respect one of our values because everyone knows Tenisha is never going to respect Sandra." The team must focus on what can be, as opposed to what has been.

The Dream It phase is divided into two steps: (1) Naming It and (2) Making the Cut. At the conclusion of this phase, the team will have an agreed upon list of 3-5 words and/or phrases describing the kind of culture they desire.

Step One: Naming It

Naming It is a process where each member of the team identifies a list of words and/or phrases describing the kind of culture they desire. This list will be used to define the team culture.

Although there are multiple ways to approach this step, I have had my most successful sessions when each team member works on his or her list individually, and then shares with the broader group. Another approach involves having the team brainstorm collectively. Whether you choose one of these routes, or come up with one of your own, here are some sample questions that can get you started.

SAMPLE QUESTIONS FOR FACILITATION

When you think about the best team you've ever been a part of, what word or phrase would you use to describe what made the team special?

If someone observed every interaction we have with each other, what words would we want them to use to describe our team?

If this was going to become the best team you have ever been a part of, what words or phrases would you use to describe the way we should relate to each other?

What words or phrases best describe the kind of culture you need to be successful?

Ask each person on the team to come up with 3-5 words or phrases. Once this is completed, have each person share their list and explain why that word/phrase is important to them. Have someone capture each word/phrase on a whiteboard or in a single document. Here is a sample of some of the words/phrases that I tend to hear when leading a team through this exercise.

Figure 8. Created by Tony Moore.

Step Two: Making the Cut

The next step is to cut the list down to a total of 3-5 words or phrases on which the team can agree. In my experience, Making the Cut is a great opportunity to stimulate discussion about team values. When handled appropriately, the process leads to clarity regarding what is truly important to the team. Acting upon this information will increase both engagement and ownership and positively impact bottom-line performance.

Imagine how much easier it will be to lead a team that has clearly articulated what is important to them and has committed to living in accordance with those values. Imagine being a part of a team where your values are aligned with the values of the people with whom you work every day. Imagine improving the employee experience by turning the experience over to the employees. Making the Cut is a giant step toward turning what you just imagined into reality.

Much like step one, there is certainly more than one way to facilitate Making the Cut. Below are a few questions to help initiate the discussion with your team, and as with the previous step, the shared information should be captured.

SAMPLE QUESTIONS FOR FACILITATION

What common themes do you see among the words/phrase? Please explain.

Are there any repeated, either literally or figuratively?

Of the themes identified, which 2-3 are most important to you? Why are they important to you?

Here are a few things to remember as you facilitate Making the Cut.

- The goal is to get down to no more than five words or phrases; more than five is too hard to manage.
- When you are looking at themes or words that appear to mean the same thing, make sure the person who provided the word or phrase agrees with the definition being used. As you will see in the next section, words have different meanings for different people.
- This is a process, so do not rush it. Increasing buy-in requires everyone to have an opportunity to participate.
- This step is called Making the Cut, so some words/phrases won't make it to the final list. The goal is to compile a list of the "most important" ones.

QUESTIONS FOR REFLECTION

How well-written are your organization's values?

Do you believe team values should be reflective of the organization's values? Why or why not?

Is it possible to share the same values as the organization, but have those values differ in the way they are expressed from team to team?

What problems might arise if one team expresses the same values differently than another team?

What might be an advantage of teams having the freedom to express values differently than other teams?

Figure 9. Photo credit deposit photos. Meme created by Tony Moore.

CHAPTER 5

DESIGN IT

Words conjure up images and stories which have emotions attached. These images, stories, and emotions serve as filters which can impact how we interpret events and experiences, as well as another's intentions. Consequently, misunderstandings frequently occur as a result of the differences of interpretation versus what actually happens in any given situation. To complicate matters even further, there is also a relationship between the meanings we ascribe to words, and the behaviors we expect to see in relation to these words. Therefore, behavioral expectations vary widely from person to person. For example, what means respect to one person may be seen as disrespect to another person.

I experienced all of this first hand when I was leading the people side of a merger. All of the factors pointed to the merger being a good deal for both companies. The two companies had similar missions, which indicated there should be great synergy.

Financially, both companies were strong, and together they would be able to capture economies of scale. Furthermore, each company enjoyed a sterling reputation which would lead to positive attention from the media, our respective communities, and prospective donors.

This deal made sense on all fronts. Equally important was what appeared to be a values alignment. There were words and phrases within our separate values statements that were so eerily similar, you would have thought the same person wrote them. Words like respect, honesty, and transparency were at the foundation of our culture, and they appeared to be at the heart of their culture also.

As I mentioned earlier, it is not just the differences in meaning we ascribe to certain words that can cause problems, but also the behaviors we expect to see in relation to those words. On paper, the values of both companies were aligned; however, the differences emerged based on how each organization demonstrated the values. One of the places this occurred was with the identified value of honesty.

Our company prided itself on being candid. The phrase

"speak the truth, even if your voice shakes" was a well-embedded mantra in our culture. We understood that sometimes the truth could be painful to hear. However, as a company, we believed there was value in being honest. While we certainly would consider the person's feelings, we would still say what we believed had to be said.

The merging company also understood truth could be painful to hear. Because of this, they gave great consideration to how this "truth" would make the recipient feel. For them, concern for the person's feelings served as a filter that ultimately determined what they would say, or if they would say anything.

Following the merger, we surveyed them about their experience with us. We expected information that would reflect the way we saw ourselves: honest, helpful, and respectful. Unfortunately, they used words like obnoxious, inconsiderate, and disrespectful. Could we be both honest, helpful, and respectful while also being obnoxious, inconsiderate, and disrespectful?

Figure 10. Photo credit deposit photos.

The answer is yes! It depends on the lens through which you interpret the behaviors you see. Because each person possesses a unique lens, there can be multiple interpretations of the same event. The values were similar in words, but the expected behaviors based on those values differed greatly.

Figure 11. Photo credit "My Wife and My Mother-in-Law" William Ely Hill

At some point, you likely have seen the above picture. When you look at it, what do you see? An old woman? A young woman? Both?

Having read Steven Covey's book, *The 7 Habits of Highly Effective People*, I became intrigued by an experiment he mentioned involving this image, so fascinated in fact, that I tried the experiment myself. During a fall semester, I was a guest lecturer at the University of Tampa's Sykes College of Business. I had the privilege of speaking to two undergraduate classes. In each case I presented half the class with a sketch of a young woman (on the left below) while the other half of the class was shown a sketch of an old woman (on the right below). After 10 seconds, I asked everyone to turn their sketches over and I revealed the original illustration of the old and young woman combined and asked what they saw.

Figure 12. Photo credit "My Wife and My Mother-in-Law" William Ely Hill

Nearly every person who first viewed the sketch of the young woman reported seeing the young woman in the combined drawing. Additionally, nearly every individual who first viewed the sketch of the old woman reported seeing an old woman in the completed drawing. What occurred during those 10 seconds is referred to as "priming" by psychologists. It is an effect in which exposure to one stimulus influences the response to another stimulus (Nugent, 2013).

Essentially, throughout our lives, we are all exposed to various forms of priming. Our priming paradigm develops based on things like the belief systems of our families, our neighborhoods, our experiences with authority figures, the schools we attend, books and magazines we read, as well as television shows. This priming creates a unique lens which we then use to interpret the events of our lives. This is why two people witnessing the same event can reach vastly different conclusions. Therefore, because of this unique lens, the goal of the Design It phase is to agree upon which behaviors best represent the values that a company has selected as central to its culture. The agreed-upon behaviors become what I call the team's "Rules of Engagement."

Rules of Engagement

Although frequently unspoken and rarely written down, all teams have Rules of Engagement. These practices define how and when team members interact, how disagreements are addressed, the tone and tenor of meetings, and a whole host of other factors. Because I believe team culture is far too important to be left up to good intentions, in using the 4D System, you and your team will not only define which behaviors are acceptable (and by default, which ones are unacceptable), but these behaviors will then be tied to your agreed-upon values. As an example, if the phrase "we have each other's backs" is selected, you need to reach an agreement on behaviors that demonstrate "we have each other's backs."

By agreeing on a set of behaviors, you increase the chances people will live according to their values while decreasing the opportunity for misinterpretation. Remember, everyone interprets the world through his or her own unique lens and it is that unique interpretation that can lead to misunderstanding. Allow me to demonstrate why this is important.

In my family, both gratefulness and honesty are important values. If someone gives you a gift, you are supposed to demonstrate gratefulness. If they ask, "Do you like it?" you then have permission to say yes or no. As a matter of fact, you are expected to tell the truth. Being honest under those circumstances is not seen as ungrateful.

MATTERS OF CULTURE
In many ways, an organization is a grouping of unique lenses that have been adjusted to see and interpret events in a similar way.

My friend, speaker and author Jessica Stollings, grew up in a family where gratefulness and honesty are also important values. In Jessica's family, if someone gives you a gift, you are expected to show gratefulness just like you are in mine. If, however, they ask, "Do you like it?" you are expected to say yes, because to do otherwise would be considered ungrateful and rude.

Now, imagine for a second that Jessica and I were on a team where gratefulness and honesty were identified as core values. Can you imagine the hurt she would feel the first time she gave me a gift and I answered the question "Do you like it?" with a "No, it's really not my style"?

So even though we share values, the behaviors that support these values are vastly different. Simply agreeing on values will never be enough to build a healthy team culture; you also need to identify the specific behaviors that support those values.

MATTERS OF CULTURE
Everyone interprets the world through their own unique lens and it is that unique lens which can lead to misunderstandings.

As an example, when one of my teams walked through this process, we decided the phrase "No Drama Zone" would be one of our values. In other words, we wanted a team in which there would not be any drama. To support this value, we came up with the following three behaviors:

1. **Deal with problems as they occur** – the commitment was to never let problems fester. It was okay to think about it overnight, or address it when you were at a better place emotionally, but you had to address it.

2. **Always speak to the person with whom you have a problem** – the commitment was to never go around the office telling everyone you had been wronged. You were committing to speaking with the person who wronged you. It was certainly okay to vent, but you had to speak to the person and allow them an opportunity to make it right.

3. **Never allow anyone to pass their drama on to you** – if someone shared with you that they had been wronged, you were committing to listening and then sending them to the person who wronged them.

I don't believe any team can work together without drama occasionally rearing its ugly head. However, on that team we were able to keep it to a minimum by following our Rules of Engagement.

Creating Rules of Engagement

The creation of Rules of Engagement is fundamental to a

healthy team culture. The process of creating Rules of Engagement involves two steps: first, identify specific behaviors, and second, reach a collective agreement on which behaviors direct the team's values. The process is very similar to what the team did during the Dream It phase. At the conclusion of this Rules of Engagement phase, each team value will have been assigned its own set of corresponding behaviors.

Although there are multiple ways to facilitate the creation of a team's Rules of Engagement, I have found that in order to gain the specificity that is critical to a culture change, the team needs laser focus on one value at a time. This allows them to identify behaviors and reach an agreement before moving on to the next value.

Step One: Identifying Behaviors

Taking each value one at a time, ask each member of the team to write down three behaviors they believe best exemplify a value from the Dream It phase. If, for instance, respect is one of your values, each team member will identify three behaviors that demonstrate respect.

I have found that providing a bit of structure is sometimes helpful. To demonstrate, the leader can provide one of the following sentences, requesting the team fill in the blanks.

SAMPLE QUESTIONS FOR FACILITATION

I believe respect is best demonstrated by _____,
_____, and _____.

I feel respected when the members of my team _____,
_____, and _____.

Once everyone has an opportunity to write down their three behaviors, have each person share their list, explain the behavior, and explain why it is important to them. Have a team member capture the information on a whiteboard or in a single document.

Step Two: Agreeing on Behaviors

Now, working from the list of suggested behaviors, the next step is to pare the list down to a total of 1-3 behaviors on which the team can agree. Be prepared for a significant amount of discussion as everyone needs to be heard. Here are some questions to help facilitate this process with your team.

SAMPLE QUESTIONS FOR FACILITATION

What common themes do you see among the behaviors? Please explain.

Are there any that are repeated, either literally or figuratively?

Of the themes identified, which 2-3 would have the most impact on our team? Why would it be important for our team to be impacted this way?

There are a few items to keep in mind as you go through this process with your team.

- The goal is to reduce the list of behaviors down to the 1-3 most important ones on which the team can agree.
- The behaviors need to be specific and observable.
- When you are identifying common themes, make sure the person who suggested the behavior agrees with the team's interpretation.
- Walk through each value one at a time, identifying behaviors and reaching agreement before moving on. Do not rush the process.

Benefits of Rules of Engagement

You are going to discover there are multiple benefits to creating Rules of Engagement. Something truly magical happens when we engage in behaviors that are aligned with our values. Below are a few benefits I have experienced in the years I have walked through this process with my teams.

Build Team Cohesion: Rules of Engagement provide your team with something around which they can rally. They have defined who they want to be as a team, and now they can work together to bring those desires to fruition. The process creates a sense of belonging, shared purpose, and accountability to one another.

Clarify Expectations: Rules of Engagement define acceptable and unacceptable behavior, reducing the chances of a misunderstanding regarding expectations.

Increase Engagement: It is commonly accepted that people do not leave jobs, they leave people. Frequently, this occurs because of the employee experience. Rules of Engagement empower team members to take control of their experience. Employees now have ownership for the kind of culture they want to have; the result of this ownership is increased engagement.

Provide a Framework for Resolving Issues: No one lives out the rules perfectly, nor is it expected they will. However, when there is a violation, you can use the agreed-upon rules to discuss the issue. In many ways, they make the discussion less personal and invite course correction.

Increase Trust: Trust remains a cornerstone of any healthy culture. Without it, a team will quickly disintegrate into self-preservation mode. Rules of Engagement provide a means for consistency between what is said and what is done, thus increasing trust.

Creating Externally-Focused Rules of Engagement

Rules of Engagement can also serve to guide your team in how to serve customers and/or interact with other departments within the organization. These externally-focused Rules of Engagement can be equally as beneficial as internally-focused ones.

Previously, I shared with you the story of walking through this process with an HR team I was leading. If you recall, the feedback indicated we had lost credibility with our customers, which in that case were other employees and departments within the organization. For that reason, we decided to create a set of externally-focused Rules of Engagement. Using the same process I described earlier, we explored a series of questions like the ones below.

SAMPLE QUESTIONS FOR FACILITATION

What would we like our coworkers to say about us as a department?

What words would we like our coworkers to use to describe their experience working with us?

Why would we want to be described this way?

Once we decided what we wanted our coworkers to say, we created a list of behaviors designed to change their perception of us. We also implemented process changes to better align the support we provided with what we wanted our coworkers' experiences to be.

To give you an example, we decided we wanted our

coworkers to see us as responsive. We identified three behaviors we believed would increase the chances we would be seen as responsive. First, we would respond to all calls and emails within 24 hours. Second, if we were unable to answer their concern immediately, we would let them know when we would have an answer. Third, if at any point we were unable to abide by the rule, we would enlist the help of another team member.

Once we created these externally-focused rules, we informed our customers, thereby setting a clear expectation. Additionally, we asked our customers to provide ongoing feedback. One year after making this commitment, we surveyed our customers and learned that they, indeed, saw us as responsive.

Figure 13. Photo credit deposit photos. Meme created by Tony Moore.

CHAPTER 6

DEVELOP IT

Break the Glasses

If you remember Maurice from earlier in the book, one of the reasons he had been allowed to operate with such a high rate of voluntary turnover was because he had continued to hit his numbers. His performance outcomes legitimized his excuses for why his employees kept leaving. The second reason he had been allowed to operate with high voluntary turnover was because the higher up in the organization you sit, the more rose-colored your glasses become. From where his superiors sat, Maurice's world looked pretty good.

This is not an uncommon phenomenon in organizations. Unfortunately, as leaders, our rose-colored glasses can prevent us from seeing our culture as it really is. This is especially the case when we have personally invested in the creation of the culture. The commitment of time and energy, as well as the accompanying stories from those early days when we were building the culture, have a hypnotic effect that can leave us frozen in time. Even when faced with evidence to the contrary, the stories we tell ourselves can both suspend reality or merge realities.

To leverage the competitive advantage that a strong culture provides, you must break the glasses and confront the brutal facts about the current state of affairs. The Develop It phase provides an opportunity to take an honest look at the gap that exists between who you are, and who you would like to become. Additionally, you must accept the reality that to start something new, you must be willing to give up something old.

Jill's Story

At one point, I worked with a leader named Jill, who was serving on the executive leadership team of her organization. Because of her length of service, she held a great deal of institutional knowledge. She was everyone's "go-to" person. She always knew how things had been done, which led to the conclusion that she knew how they *should* be done.

Jill also played another role on her team: she did everyone's work for them. When deadlines were in jeopardy of not being met, Jill would strap on her superhero costume and ensure the work got done. When questioned about this role she played, she was famous for saying, "It's easier for me to just do it than take the time to re-explain it to them." This ritual of doing work for her team played out over and over again—as would her proclamation that she had too much work.

When we surveyed her team, an interesting theme emerged. Rather than seeing Jill as helpful, they viewed her as a micromanager and difficult to please. What she saw as "it's easier to do it myself," they saw as an unwillingness to help them increase their competency.

In our work together, the team decided one of their core values would be, "Everyone carries their own weight, but asks for help when needed." Everyone, and especially Jill, believed this would be a good fit for the team. From Jill's perspective, she could accomplish more if she did not have to do everyone else's work for them. As she put it, "I need to start leading and get out of the weeds."

What Jill did not count on was how much pleasure she derived from being everyone's go-to person. Being the person who always got it done made her feel valued and needed. In order to truly embrace "everyone carries their own weight, but asks for help when needed," Jill would have to adopt a new behavior by giving up the old. More importantly, she would have to find other ways to fulfill that most basic of human needs: the need to feel valued.

There are multiple challenges you will face when leading a culture change, and nowhere do these challenges become more evident than in the Develop It phase. As mentioned, the first two phases are aspirational in nature. In fact, there is a "feel good" element that accompanies Dream It and Design It. However, during Develop It, the rubber hits the road. It is one thing to speak of managerial courage, defined as a willingness to speak truth in the face of opposition. It is a completely different matter to demonstrate managerial courage on a team where this has historically been viewed as divisive, uncooperative, and led to comments such as "she is not a team player."

Before we delve into the challenge, there are a few issues I would like to mention. First and foremost, while every member of the team must be committed to the process, their hearts must long for the outcome. As someone once wrote, "If you want to build a ship, don't drum up people to collect wood, and don't assign them tasks and work, but rather teach them to long for the endless immensity of the sea."

The prospect of being a part of a team whose behavior is aligned with its values must remain a primary motivator. The thought of improving bottom-line performance by creating a culture of engagement and ownership must be at the forefront of each team member's mind. The ability not only to define the employee experience they desire, but the opportunity to make it a reality, will get the team through the challenges ahead.

Secondly, everyone must remember that this is a process, and behavior change takes time. For that reason, patience is the order of the day. Do not expect change to occur overnight; be willing to extend benefit of the doubt.

Third, to quote my dear friend, David Dennis, "If you want to change the world, start where you are and work your way out." Everyone must start by addressing their own challenge and soliciting the assistance of their peers before they point out the shortcomings of others.

Finally, as mentioned previously, when the team makes a commitment to start something new, they are also making a commitment to give up something old. Normally, I believe old habits rarely die; they tend to simply hibernate. So don't be surprised when old behaviors resurface. Habits, well-established rituals, and ways of thinking and responding must all be confronted in order to take on the new behaviors. Without this confrontation, no lasting culture change can occur. Therefore, own it, apologize if necessary, recommit, and move on.

MATTERS OF CULTURE

When the team makes a commitment to start something new, they are also making a commitment to give up something old.

Individual Challenges

During the Develop It phase, individual challenges refer to those things each member of the team will need to give up in order to live out the newly established values. Much like Jill's story, this is sometimes easier said than done. Remember, these are habits, rituals, and ways of thinking and responding that are either in conflict with the Rules of Engagement, or make it challenging to live by the Rules of Engagement. This process requires a high degree of self-reflection, something that can be very difficult due to our natural inclination to see ourselves in a favorable light.

Figure 14. Photo credit deposit photos.

There is a great verse in the Bible that sums the challenge up nicely: "Every way of a man is right in his own eyes ..." (Proverbs 21:2a, Crossway Bibles, 2007). As a leader and someone who has worked with leaders over the course of my career, I have seen this phenomenon play out multiple times. It is this viewpoint that must be addressed.

Fundamentally, I have found there is an inextricable link between your team's ability to successfully embed these values and the degree to which they are willing to be honest about their individual challenges. Self-examination requires a great deal of courage and revealing what you have discovered takes both courage and trust. Because of that, I would like to share a couple of different options to facilitate this phase of the process. These are merely suggestions; feel free to approach it as you and the team deem best. As you consider the different approaches, here are a few questions that can be used to further the process:

SAMPLE QUESTIONS FOR FACILITATION

Which one of our Rules of Engagement will be most challenging for you and what makes it difficult? What one thing can you do to overcome this challenge?

Are there certain situations where you would find it more difficult than others to follow one or more of the Rules of Engagement? What are these situations and what can you do to overcome these challenges?

Is there anyone on the team with whom you will find it difficult to follow the Rules of Engagement? What steps can you take to overcome this challenge?

Have each person complete these statements:

In order to make these Rules of Engagement a reality, I need to stop _____.

In order to make these Rules of Engagement a reality, I need to start _____.

In order to make these Rules of Engagement a reality, I need to continue _____.

As mentioned, there are multiple ways to address individual challenges. Remember, the goal is to encourage self-reflection with each member of the team identifying the changes they need to make in order to live by the Rules of Engagement. Here are a few approaches I have taken.

Discovery Partners

Give each member of the team an index card. On one side of the card, have them write the one rule that will present the greatest challenge for them and the reason(s) why it will be challenging. On the flip side of the card, have them write one or more things they can do to overcome the challenge. Have each person place their card in an envelope, seal it, write the name of someone they trust on the front of the envelope. After the meeting, they are to give their envelope to the person whose name is on the front. This can be someone who is or isn't on the team. However, it works best when the person is on the team. The person who receives the envelope is to open it in 30 days, read what's on the card, and reach out to the person who gave them the envelope to inquire how faithful they have been in taking steps to overcome the challenge.

Here is an example of how the index card activity might play out. Imagine if one of the team values was "Embrace Conflict Resolution." If you were someone who tends to shy away from conflict, you would write this value and your challenge on one side of the index card. On the flip side of the card, you would list things you could do to overcome the challenge of embracing conflict resolution. You might, for example, commit to reading a book on the subject, attend training, or seek out a coach or mentor who is good at conflict resolution.

Two Heads Are Better Than One

In the second approach, each person takes out a piece of paper and writes the one rule that will present the greatest challenge for them and the reason(s) why it will be challenging. Divide the team into groups of 2-3. One at a time, have each person share what they wrote on their paper. Their partner(s) will then suggest things they can do to overcome the challenge. Be sure to allow sufficient time for suggestions and discussion.

If time allows, a great addition to this exercise is to allow anyone who is comfortable to share their challenge and the feedback they received with the entire team. This will enable other members of the team to also make suggestions.

Putting It All on the Table

The third approach uses one of the suggested questions above or one you deem to be more impactful. Have individual team members take turns sharing their answers with the entire group. Once an individual has shared his or her answer to the question, members of the team suggest ways they can overcome the challenge.

This approach has the power to really transform the team by deepening their relationships with one another. When handled properly, it creates transparency and facilitates trust and dependence on others while also providing a reminder that everyone is human. At the same time, it is important to remember this approach requires team members to display a high level of vulnerability. For that reason, only those people who are comfortable sharing should do so.

Group Challenges

Besides individual challenges, group challenges may exist as well. Group challenges focus on policies, practices, and processes that are in conflict with your Rules of Engagement. If not in direct conflict, they are policies, practices, or processes that will make it challenging to live in accordance with the Rules of Engagement.

As an example, I was working at an organization where we took some very deliberate and intentional steps to define the behaviors that would support our values. We started with our Executive Leadership Team who in turn trained all their directors from across the organization. These directors then trained their teams. It was a massive, successful undertaking. Although it took several years with weekly focus before we saw the fruit of our labor in full bloom, we began to see the culture shift after only a few months. The intense focus gave everyone in the organization something to talk about. Some of the talk was positive and some was negative, but everyone was talking.

About 18 months into establishing this new culture, we encountered the first real challenge to one of our organization's policies. There was an employee who had to take time off work because her child was ill and had to be hospitalized. She quickly exhausted her Paid Time Off (PTO) but still needed time off work to be with her child. Needless to say, she could not afford to be without a paycheck.

MATTERS OF CULTURE

Where policies, practices, and processes can be changed, it is critical that you make the changes. In situations where they cannot be changed, do not pretend as if they are not in conflict. Admit they are and be honest about the fact that they cannot be changed. You will lose credibility if you pretend otherwise.

Several of her coworkers contacted our benefits team to see if they could donate their PTO to her. It was a wonderfully thoughtful gesture, yet we were not set up to fulfill their request. To the casual observer it seems simple: I have PTO; she needs PTO. What's the problem? In reality, it's not as simple as it appears on the surface. PTO has a dollar amount attached which varies based on the employee's hourly wage. Because of this difference in wages, one person's PTO might be valued differently than another's. Simply moving hours from one person to another is an accounting nightmare. Because of that fact, these employees were told it could not be done.

Au contraire! Her coworkers' response was swift, simple, and direct. "How can we say caring is one of our values but deny this employee in her time of need?" They were right, and their approach not only resulted in a donation to the employee, but also resulted in the creation of a PTO donation bank.

MATTERS OF CULTURE

If you want to know where the inconsistencies are in your culture, ask the employees who sit furthest down the organizational chart.

In order to examine group challenges surrounding policies, practices, and processes that conflict with your Rules of Engagement, consider the following questions.

SAMPLE QUESTIONS FOR FACILITATION

What are the policies, practices, or processes that need to change in order to create alignment with the Rules of Engagement?

What new policies, practices, or processes should you implement because they demonstrate the Rules of Engagement?

What cultural norms on your team will impede your ability to create the new culture? What steps are needed to change these norms?

Have each person fill in the following blanks:

In order to make these Rules of Engagement a reality, we need to stop _____.

In order to make these Rules of Engagement a reality, we need to start _____.

In order to make these Rules of Engagement a reality, we need to continue _____.

Needless to say, the Develop It phase is strategically significant to a healthy, productive culture. This phase requires a commitment to the brutally honest evaluation of each individual and the team as a whole. Challenges during the Develop It phase will provide opportunities for your team to gain trust and create alignment between what you say you believe and what you do.

QUESTIONS FOR REFLECTION

This phase requires brutal honesty. Do you believe the team will find it difficult to be honest? Why or why not?

What steps could the team take in preparation for Develop It that would increase the degree of honesty?

What do you need from the team in order to be more honest?

What one thing can you do to increase the chances team members will be honest?

"... courage is the most important of all the virtues. Because without courage, you cannot practice any other virtue consistently."

Maya Angelou

Figure 15. Photo credit deposit photos. Meme created by Tony Moore.

CHAPTER 7

DEFEND IT

For a period of time, my family and I were living in South Bend, Indiana. I needed to travel to Fort Wayne, Indiana, on business, so I loaded up my car and headed out. About 30-35 miles into the trip, I decided to stop in Middlebury, the next town I would enter, and get something to drink.

I passed up a not-so-clean-looking convenience store in favor of a grocery store with which I was familiar. I parked my car and as I was headed to the door, I saw something I had never seen before: a sign in a special section of the parking lot that read *Horse and Buggy Parking Only.*

I have to tell you, in light of the fact that it was 2004, I was having a hard time wrapping my head around the need for such a parking space. Think about it. 35 miles to the west was Notre Dame University, one of the world's most prestigious learning institutions, and here where I stood was a parking space for a horse and buggy. I later learned there were Amish communities in and around the Middlebury area, so then the space made more sense.

Well, you may have heard about a group of Amish people who pulled up stakes from a settlement in the Midwest and relocated to a remote area in Peru. When asked their reason for doing so, one of them responded, "We got tired of having to move our wagons over to the side of the road to let the cars go by" (Van Ekeren, 2000).

Now, my Amish brothers and sisters have some deeply-held beliefs about the usage of technology like automobiles, so I understand the decision. On the other hand, there are plenty of non-Amish people who do the equivalent of pulling over to the side of the road to let cars go by, rather than change.

Granted, changing behavior is very difficult to do. I once read of a Canadian neurosurgeon who discovered when a person is forced to change a fundamental belief, the sensations in the brain are the same as enduring torture (Van Ekeren, 2000). I do not know if that is true; however, this research would certainly explain some of the challenges I have experienced over the course of my career when leading change.

Create a New Normal

Once you have gotten the team's commitment to change the culture and taken deliberate steps to create a new culture of engagement and ownership, the focus shifts to making the changes stick. Making them stick can be very difficult to do. Coincidentally, an introduction of change into the culture is very similar to what happens in the human body when an infection enters it. The red blood cells (the old habits) attack the infection (the new culture) in a quest to return to homeostasis.

Whatever cultural norms, habits, rituals, or behaviors have been the norm, members of your team will attempt to replicate. As I mentioned before, this is primarily because old habits do not die, they simply hibernate. Moreover, the responsibility of supporting the change rests with the team that dreamt, designed, and developed the new culture.

The primary objective in the Defend It phase is to construct opportunities to deeply embed the new values and practices into the team culture, thereby creating a new normal. Although this may be arduous, remember, a rewarding culture of engagement is within your grasp. The following are five tools I have found useful in executing and sustaining culture change.

Build Team Rituals

One of the best ways to sustain change is by building rituals. In their book *The Power of Full Engagement*, Jim Loehr and Tony Schwartz (2003) reference research that seems to indicate "… as little as 5% of our behaviors are consciously self-directed. We are creatures of habit, and as much as 95% of what we do occurs automatically, or in reaction to a demand or an anxiety." In other words, most of what we do is based on rituals. To the extent we can consciously build new rituals, "they will reduce the need to rely on our limited conscious will and discipline to take action … rituals are a powerful means by which to translate our values and priorities into action …"

Following are some suggestions to get started:

Ask Your Team: I have found the best ideas always come from my team. Who better to come up with rituals to sustain change than the people who actually need to sustain the change?

Deep Dive a Value: Select one value per quarter to discuss during a team meeting. Before the meeting, provide the value to be discussed and a question to start the conversation. Consider a few sample questions based on respect:

SAMPLE QUESTIONS FOR FACILITATION

Why is respect important to you?

How do you typically respond when you feel disrespected?

What is one thing the team can do to demonstrate "we respect you?"

What happens to team morale when everyone respects each other?

For you, is respect something that is earned, or is it something you give automatically when you first meet a new person?

Can respect be regained once it is lost? Why or why not?

Plan a Team Outing: Once or twice a year, plan a team outing that converts your values into action. If you have a team value such as "think of others before you think of yourself," volunteering at a homeless shelter, local food bank, or thrift store is a great way to put this value into action.

Give Your Values a Heartbeat: Each year, choose a local charity to support. Volunteer your time and your talents, or engage in activities that increase awareness or raise money. Be sure the support you are providing is aligned with your values. The goal is to create a connection between what you believe and what you do.

Start a Book Club: Each year, pick a book related to your values and have everyone read it. Set aside time during your team meeting to discuss a chapter, paragraph, or excerpt.

Recognition and Reward: Create a program to recognize team members who demonstrate the values. I have found that programs like these work best when team members nominate each other. The program is more about recognition than the reward, so keep it simple. Find something that can be passed from winner to winner and displayed at their workstations. Once again, ask the team for ideas.

Display Values in Plain Sight: There are a multitude of ways to keep your Rules of Engagement front and center. I have always had an affinity for laminated copies at everyone's desk. You can also have these made into posters and hang them throughout the office.

Hire for Values Alignment

To sustain cultural change, you need a process for ensuring team values are shared with every potential new team member. During the interview process, share the values and the reasons why they are important. Whatever current hiring process you are using, be sure to incorporate questions related to your team values, and only hire people with whom these values resonate. Here are a few examples for your team.

1. Which one of these values resonates the most with you and why?

2. Give me an example of a time you demonstrated one of these values in the workplace.

3. Give me an example of a time when you failed to demonstrate one of these values in the workplace. What did you do afterwards?

Take Your Newbies to School

Once a person is hired, it is critically important to spend time discussing team values and Rules of Engagement with the new team member. Taking your newbies to school is a critical part of sustaining change.

I have found it beneficial to not only make this discussion a part of the orientation process, but to have someone from the team go over the information with the new team member. Doing so communicates that the values and Rules of Engagement are not only important to you; they are important to the team. It demonstrates that this is not a top-down, check-the-box initiative, but rather something of which the entire team has taken ownership. Imagine the impact on a new employee's feelings about their decision to join your organization when you give team expectations the same level of importance as payroll and benefits orientation, mandatory training, and reviewing the employee handbook.

Flood the Bucket

At one point in my career, I received a call from a friend of mine who had recently been appointed CEO of her organization. She knew she needed to make a lot of changes, but she wanted to ensure she didn't move too fast and risk losing the trust of her staff. Interestingly enough, one of her operations directors had been recently fired, so as she put it, "She had the perfect spot for me."

To be honest with you, I do not know when I have been asked to lead a more dysfunctional team. The infighting, backbiting, and gossiping were off the chart. I also had the good fortune of having three managers who all thought they should have been appointed to my position. To say I had my hands full is an understatement. Did I mention the CEO was a friend of mine?

Having made the mistake earlier in my career of firing nearly everyone on my team when I took over, I decided to take a more measured approach this time.

MATTERS OF CULTURE

By quickly firing a large number of people when you take over a team, you impact the trust of those who remain, even when the people you fire need to go.

After working with my team for a while, we created our Rules of Engagement. Because the organization's value statements were so well written, we used them as our own. Then we outlined the team behaviors that would support the values. I had everyone sign a copy. We had them laminated and placed at each workstation.

About 45 days later, I had a manager give her two weeks' notice. On her last day she completed an exit survey with someone in the HR department.

The next morning, I had the Director of HR waiting for me at my office. She went on to tell me how poorly I was rated on the exit survey. So low, in fact, that she had felt compelled to come see me first thing that morning.

I sat and patiently read through the comments. Interestingly enough, there was a common theme throughout. Besides the fact that the employee did not like me, she said she felt micromanaged and treated like a child. When asked for specific examples, she focused exclusively on the Rules of Engagement. "They were childish. They focused on things people should have learned in kindergarten. He actually made us sign them like we were in grade school."

After reading the comments in their entirety, I handed the results to the Director of HR and said, "I have one question for you. After she finished the survey, did she leave?"

"Yes," she replied.

To which I responded, "Mission accomplished!"

I had effectively done what David Dennis, a long-time friend, and CEO of Eckerd Connects, called flooding the bucket. David once told me the story of a young man who had grown up on a farm. The young man's father gave him the assignment of cleaning out a bucketful of manure. The young man put on a pair of gloves, grabbed the bucket, and just as he was about to reach in and start scooping it out with his hand, his father caught him and said, "What are you doing?"

The boy said, "Well, I'm going to clean this."

The father said, "Let me show you a trick." He pulled a water hose over and began to flood that dirty bucket with clean water. The more clean water he put in, the less manure remained.

The father said to his son, "You can clean the bucket out by hand, but when you finish, you will smell like manure. Flooding the bucket with clean water has the same effect without transferring the smell."

The same is true with this process. To embed these values in your team, you've got to flood the bucket. Don't go into this thinking "who do I need to get rid of?" Instead, begin to create enough positive change that people will want to remain a part of it.

So even though my team member made it about us when she completed her exit survey, the reality was we flooded the bucket with so much clean water that she couldn't stick around. We made it such a positive place that she left on her own. She wanted a place where gossip and drama were accepted practices, and our change in behavior left her no place to spread her negativity. Your goal with your team is to flood that bucket with so many good changes that people not aligned with the values will become uncomfortable.

Part Ways with Nonbelievers

As difficult as it may be to part ways with an employee, there are times when it is necessary. When you and your team are building a new culture, it is critically important that everyone be on the same page. Doing so takes time, with some adapting faster than others.

MATTERS OF CULTURE

A former CEO once told me, "In matters of style, bend like a reed. In matters of character, stand like an oak."

So how do you know who's going to adapt and who's not? The truth of the matter is, you don't. As I think back to my early days in leadership, I feel certain there were people who did not make it on my team because I didn't believe they would make it. I am not saying that my beliefs influenced their behavior. I am, however, saying that my gut feeling influenced my judgement. That, of course, is the problem with a gut feeling. Once you have one, you start looking for evidence to confirm your feeling. Only time will tell who is going to embrace the new culture, so do not try to guess.

Nevertheless, there will be times when action needs to be taken. My dear friend, colleague, and facilitator at The Strategic Change Initiative, Tom Woll, taught me a formula that can be helpful in deciding what steps to take when someone does not appear to be embracing the new direction. Tom calls his formula, "Can't, Don't, Won't." You can apply this formula to multiple employee situations.

Can't, Don't, Won't

Can't:

If they **can't do it** because they don't know how, the appropriate intervention is training so they can develop the necessary skills.

Don't:

If they **don't do it** because they haven't fully let go of old habits, the appropriate intervention is coaching and mentoring.

Won't:

If they **won't do it** because they don't believe, the appropriate intervention is to part ways with them.

Resistance is a normal response to change and should be expected. Therefore, you should be patient as you and your team attempt to create a new normal. That being said, outside of a leader failing to live by the agreed-upon values, nothing will thwart the team's efforts faster than allowing nonbelievers to stay.

:

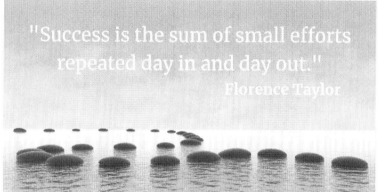

Figure 16. Photo credit deposit photos. Meme created by Tony Moore

CHAPTER 8

THE REALITY OF CULTURE CHANGE

Leading a culture change is not for the faint of heart. First of all, it takes a tremendous amount of courage to admit your team's culture needs to change. It is easier to point fingers when performance outcomes are lacking and employee turnover is high as opposed to addressing the root cause. It's less threatening to the ego to say, "I have a gossiping team" versus asking, "Why is gossip able to take root and flourish in our culture?" Leading a culture change requires honesty, transparency, and a willingness to take a long, hard look at who you are, versus who you say you are.

Secondly, changing a culture is hard work. Rituals, thinking patterns, and ways of responding are deeply ingrained and like all habits, they are difficult to overcome. Successfully executing the 4D process takes patience, persistence, and practice. It requires a willingness to accept progress over perfection and an ability to extend benefit of the doubt when old habits re-surface.

Finally, culture change is tedious work, or to quote the poet, Florence Taylor, "Success is the sum of small efforts repeated day in and day out." Culture change requires you and your team to keep their eye on the bigger picture of what you plan to accomplish while remaining faithful to taking the same small steps over and over again.

So here's the million-dollar question: are you up to the challenge? Your team, your organization, your clients, and customers deserve the very best. Culture is the soil in which everything in your organization lives or dies. A culture in 4D ensures a well-fertilized soil where your team can both grow and be empowered to accomplish the organization's mission.

Summary

ADDITIONAL WORKSHEETS

I hope this book has inspired you to help change the course of the culture within your organization. I have additional worksheets in this section to get you started. They are also available for download from my website to make it easier for you to fill out. Just visit www.tonymoorespeaks.com

DREAM IT

SAMPLE QUESTIONS FOR FACILITATION

When you think about the best team you've ever been a part of, what word or phrase would you use to describe what made the team special?

If someone observed every interaction we have with each other, what words would we want them to use to describe our team?

If this was going to become the best team you have ever been a part of, what words or phrases would you use to describe the way we relate to each other?

What words or phrases best describe the kind of culture you need to be successful?

DESIGN IT- IDENTIFYING BEHAVIORS
SAMPLE QUESTIONS FOR FACILITATION

I believe (*INSERT VALUE*) is best demonstrated by _____, _____, and _____.

I feel (*INSERT VALUE*) when the members of my team _____, _____, and _____.

DESIGN IT – AGREEING ON BEHAVIORS

SAMPLE QUESTIONS FOR FACILITATION

What common themes do you see among the behaviors? Please explain.

Are there any that are repeated, either literally or figuratively?

Of the themes identified, which 2-3 would have the most impact on our team? Why would it be important for our team to be impacted this way?

DESIGN IT – EXTERNALLY-FOCUSED RULES OF ENGAGEMENT

SAMPLE QUESTIONS FOR FACILITATION

What would we like our coworkers to say about us as a department?

What words would we like our coworkers to use to describe their experience working with us?

Why would we want to be described this way?

DEVELOP IT-

INDIVIDUAL CHALLENGES

SAMPLE QUESTIONS FOR FACILITATION

Which one of our Rules of Engagement will be most challenging for you and what will make it difficult? What one thing can you do to overcome this challenge?

Are there certain situations where you would find it more difficult than others to follow one or more of the Rules of Engagement? What are these situations and what can you do to overcome these challenges?

Is there anyone on the team with whom you will find it

difficult to follow the Rules of Engagement? What steps can you take to overcome this challenge?

Have each person complete these statements:

In order to make these Rules of Engagement a reality, I need to stop _____.

In order to make these Rules of Engagement a reality, I need to start _____.

In order to make these Rules of Engagement a reality, I need to continue _____.

DEVELOP IT-
GROUP CHALLENGES

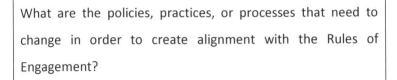

SAMPLE QUESTIONS FOR FACILITATION

What are the policies, practices, or processes that need to change in order to create alignment with the Rules of Engagement?

What new policies, practices, or processes should you implement because they demonstrate the Rules of Engagement?

What cultural norms on your team will impede your ability to create the new culture? What steps are needed to change these norms?

Have each person fill in the following blanks:

In order to make these Rules of Engagement a reality, we need to stop _____.

In order to make these Rules of Engagement a reality, we need to start _____.

In order to make these Rules of Engagement a reality, we need to continue _____.

ABOUT THE AUTHOR

Tony and his wife Aundra have been married for 21 years. They live in Florida with their daughter, Monet, son, Parker, and Tony's mother, Paulette. They are the proud owners of two dogs, a boxer named Toby, and a Lab/Rottweiler mix named Maggie. When Tony isn't cheering for his beloved Texas Longhorns or Dallas Cowboys, you will find him kayaking, snorkeling, or hanging out on the beach with a good book.

Tony is a Culture Architect, Keynote Speaker, and recovering Human Resource Executive. For more than 25 years, Tony has held leadership positions in social service agencies whose primary focus has been the health and well-being of children. Most recently, he worked for a national nonprofit organization where he helped design and build the organization's culture and led the cultural integration of multiple mergers and acquisitions.

As a leader, Tony's goal has always been the same: impact the organization by positively impacting the lives of those he leads. It was this passion to bring out the best in people that led to his entry into Talent Management and Development. Once there, he discovered he could multiply the impact of an organization's talent by creating and implementing people processes designed to support, engage, and equip those charged with the responsibility of carrying out the organization's mission. His unique blend of integrity, empathy, and energetic pursuit of change inspires confidence and lasting vision-to-implementation in every organization he touches.

Believing people are the bridge between strategy and execution, his firm Tony Moore Speaks helps organizations create a bridge-strengthening culture. Tony has a Master's in Organizational Leadership and is a SHRM Senior Certified Professional.

For more information about Tony's business, visit his website, http://tonymoorespeaks.com or contact him directly at tony@tonymoorespeaks.com.

APPENDIX

Adkins, A. (2016, January 13). Employee engagement in U.S. stagnant in 2015. *Gallup News.*

Barrett, R. (2011). *Building a values-driven organization: A whole-system approach to cultural transformation.* London: Routledge.

Covey, S. R. (2004). *The 7 habits of highly effective people: Restoring the character ethic* (Revised edition). New York, NY: Free Press.

Chambliss, D. F. (1989). The mundanity of excellence: An ethnographic report on stratification and Olympic swimmers. *Sociological Theory, 7*(1), 70-86. doi:10.2307/202063

de Bono, E. (1985). *Six thinking hats.* Boston, MA: Little, Brown and Company.

Gerstner, L. V. (2002). *Who says elephants can't dance?* N.p.: Harper Business.

H. (n.d.). *Andrew Van Buren plate spinner* [Photograph]. Image found online. Photographer's name unavailable.

Hill, W. E. (1915, November 6). *My wife and my mother-in-law* [1 photomechanical print : halftone]. Library of Congress Prints and Photographs Division Washington, D.C. 20540 USA http://www.loc.gov/rr/print/ ; no known restrictions on publication.

Kotter, J. P., & Heskett, J. L. (2011). *Corporate culture and performance*. N.p.: Free Press.

Kruse, K. (2015, December 8). How Chick-fil-A created a culture that lasts. [Online Exclusive] *Forbes*. Retrieved from https://www.forbes.com/sites/kevinkruse/2015/12/08/how-chick-fil-a-created-a-culture-that-lasts/#79de0ba33602

Loehr, J., & Schwartz, T. (2003). *The power of full engagement: Managing energy, not time, is the key to high performance and personal renewal*. N.p.: Free Press.

Newton, R. (2016, November 2). HR can't change company culture by Itself. [Online Exclusive] *Harvard Business Review*. Retrieved from https://hbr.org/2016/11/hr-cant-change-company-culture-by-itself

Nugent, P. M.S.(2013). Priming. In *Psychology Dictionary*. Retrieved from https://psychologydictionary.org/priming/ What is PRIMING? definition of PRIMING (Psychology Dictionary)

Osterwalder, A., Pigneur, Y., & Guppta, K. (2016, July 7). Don't let your company culture just happen. [Online Exclusive] *Harvard Business Review*. Retrieved from https://hbr.org/2016/07/dont-let-your-company-culture-just-happen

Smith, S. S., Peters, R., & Caldwell, C. (2016, June 14). Creating a culture of engagement -- Insights for application. *Business and Management Research*, 5(2), 70. doi:10.5430/bmr.v5n2p70

Soergel, A. (2015, December 28). 2016 could be the year of the job-hopper. *U.S. News & World Report*. Retrieved from https://www.usnews.com/news/articles/2015-12-28/2016-could-be-the-year-of-the-job-hopper

Van Ekeren, G. (2000). *Speaker's sourcebook II: Quotes, stories, and anecdotes for every occasion (Bk.2) (2nd ed.)*. New Jersey: Prentice Hall Press.

Williams, N. J., & Glisson, C. (2014, April). Testing a theory of organizational culture, climate and youth outcomes in child welfare systems: a United States national study. *Child Abuse Negl.*, 38(4), 757-767. doi:10.1016/j.chiabu.2013.09.003